A Tree Stands Tall

CARRIE BELL HARRELL-WINNS

Gotham Books

30 N Gould St.
Ste. 20820, Sheridan, WY 82801
https://gothambooksinc.com/

Phone: 1 (307) 464-7800

© 2025 *Carrie Bell Harrell-Winns*. All rights reserved.

No part of this book may be reproduced, stored in a retrieval system, or transmitted by any means without the written permission of the author.

Published by Gotham Books (February 19, 2025)

ISBN: 979-8-3485-1758-8 (H)
ISBN: 979-8-3485-1755-7 (P)
ISBN: 979-8-3485-1756-4 (E)

Because of the dynamic nature of the Internet, any web addresses or links contained in this book may have changed since publication and may no longer be valid.

The views expressed in this work are solely those of the author and do not necessarily reflect the views of the publisher, and the publisher hereby disclaims any responsibility for them.

In Loving Memory of:

**The Late
Rev. Thomas S. Lance
&
Sis. Floraine
Canteen Lance**

**The Late
Major J. Miller
"Uncle D"**

In the midst of the street of it, and on either side of the river, was there the tree of life, which bare twelve manner of fruits, and yielded her fruit every month: and the leaves of the tree were for the healing of the nations.

Revelation 22:2

Blessed are they that do his commandments, that they may have right to the tree of life, and may enter in through the gates into the city.

Revelation 22:14

He that hath an ear, let him hear what the Spirit saith unto the churches; To him that overcometh will I give to eat of the tree of life, which is in the midst of the paradise of God.

Revelation 2:7

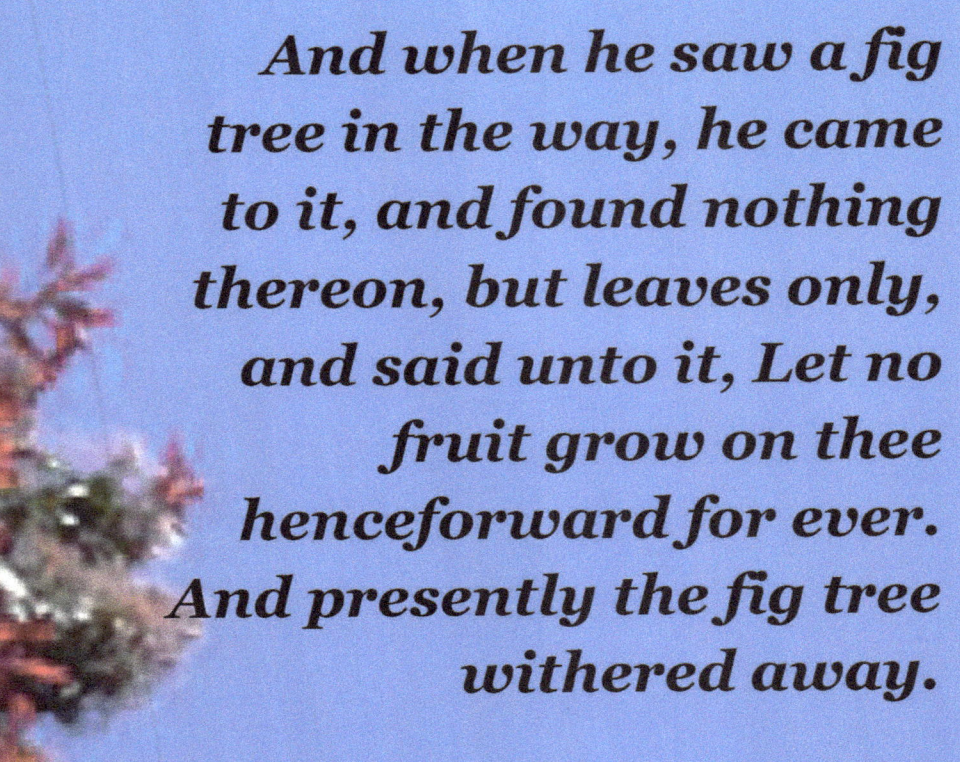

And when he saw a fig tree in the way, he came to it, and found nothing thereon, but leaves only, and said unto it, Let no fruit grow on thee henceforward for ever. And presently the fig tree withered away.

Matthew 21:19

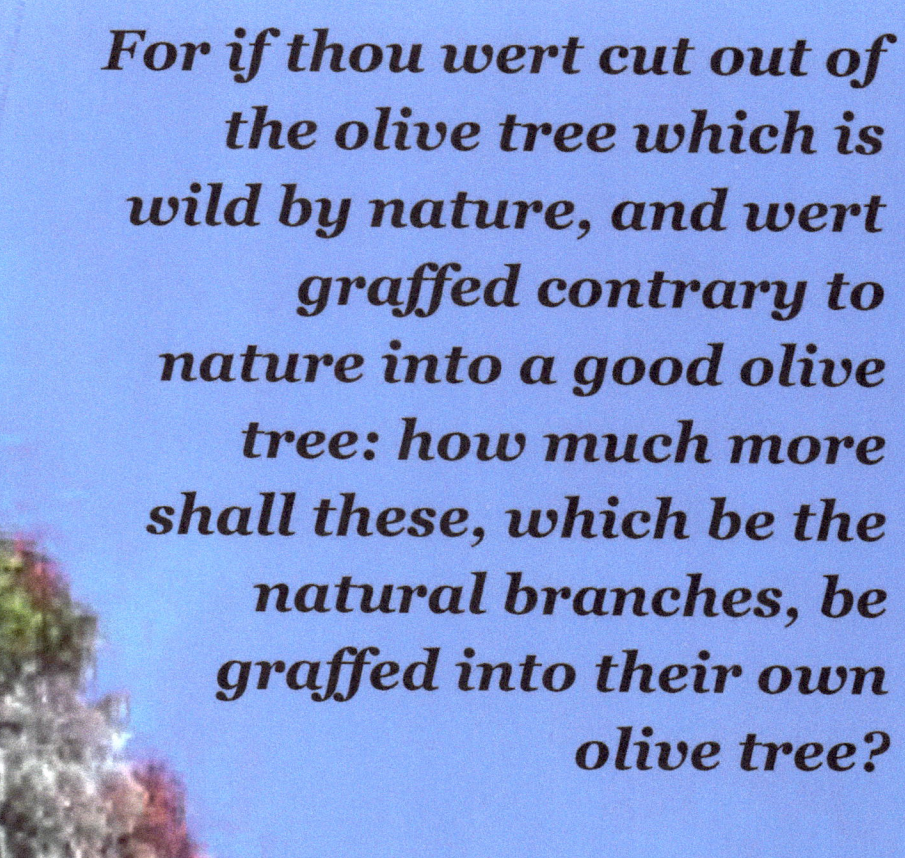

For if thou wert cut out of the olive tree which is wild by nature, and wert graffed contrary to nature into a good olive tree: how much more shall these, which be the natural branches, be graffed into their own olive tree?

Romans 11:24

And if some of the branches be broken off, and thou, being a wild olive tree, wert graffed in among them, and with them partakest of the root and fatness of the olive tree;

Romans 11:17

For a good tree bringeth not forth corrupt fruit; neither doth a corrupt tree bring forth good fruit.

Luke 6:43

Even so every good tree bringeth forth good fruit; but a corrupt tree bringeth forth evil fruit.

Matthew 7:17

A good tree cannot bring forth evil fruit, neither can a corrupt tree bring forth good fruit.

Matthew 7:18

Either make the tree good, and his fruit good; or else make the tree corrupt, and his fruit corrupt: for the tree is known by his fruit.

Matthew 12:33

For if they do these things in a green tree, what shall be done in the dry?

Luke 23:31

And when the disciples saw it, they marvelled, saying, How soon is the fig tree withered away!

Matthew 21:20

And he ran before, and climbed up into a sycamore tree to see him: for he was to pass that way.

Luke 19:4

And in the morning, as they passed by, they saw the fig tree dried up from the roots.

Mark 11:20

And he spake to them a parable; Behold the fig tree, and all the trees;

Luke 21:29

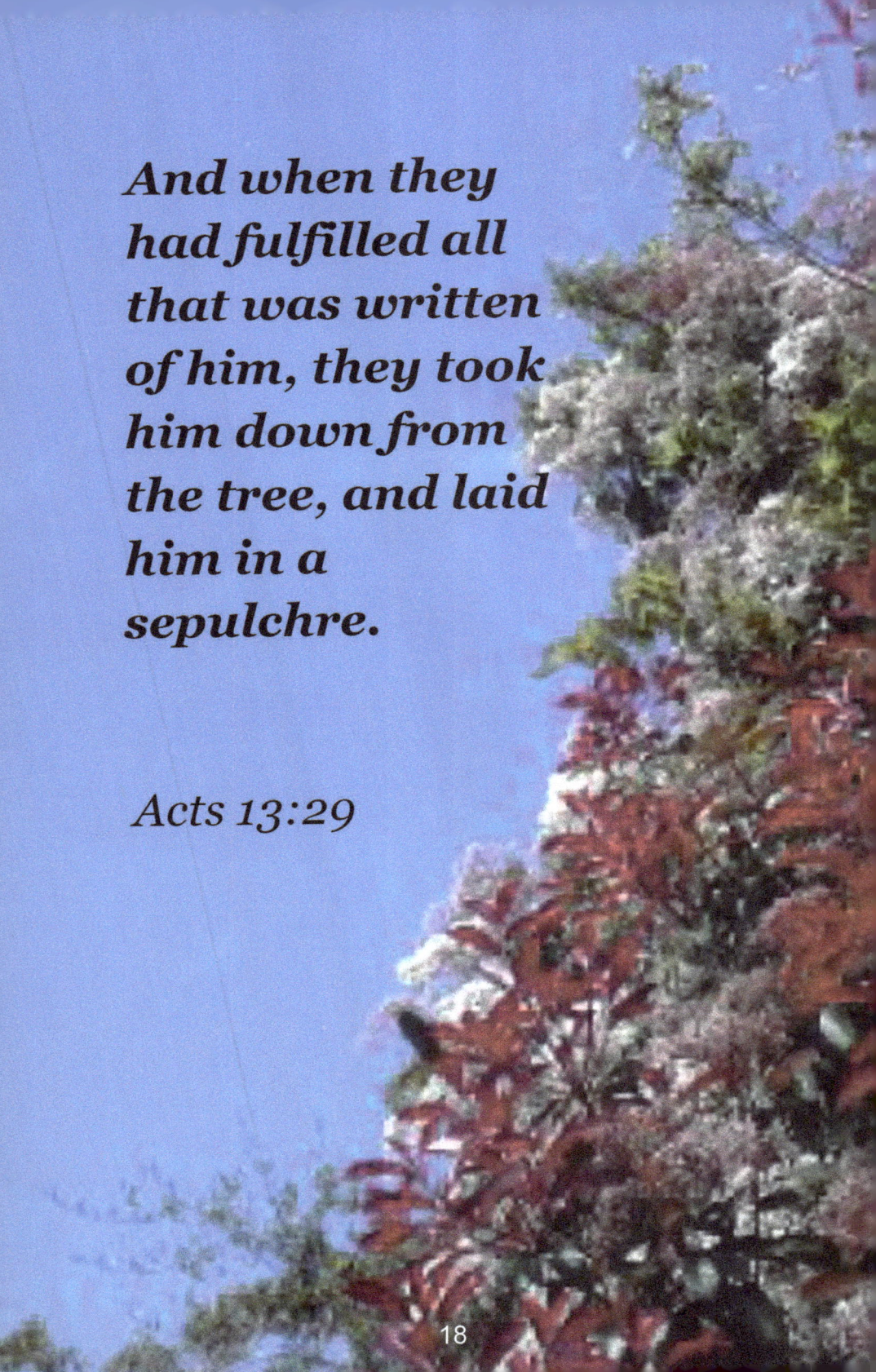

And when they had fulfilled all that was written of him, they took him down from the tree, and laid him in a sepulchre.

Acts 13:29

The God of our fathers raised up Jesus, whom ye slew and hanged on a tree.

Acts 5:30

Every tree that bringeth not forth good fruit is hewn down, and cast into the fire.

Matthew 7:19

Now learn a parable of the fig tree; When her branch is yet tender, and putteth forth leaves, ye know that summer is near:

Mark 13:28

And we are witnesses of all things which he did both in the land of the Jews, and in Jerusalem; whom they slew and hanged on a tree:

Acts 10:39

Then the devil leaveth him, and, behold, angels came and ministered unto him.

Matthew 4:11

The enemy that sowed them is the devil; the harvest is the end of the world; and the reapers are the angels.

Matthew 13:39

But when Herod was dead, behold, an angel of the Lord appeareth in a dream to Joseph in Egypt.

Matthew 2:19

And saith unto him, If thou be the Son of God, cast thyself down: for it is written, He shall give his angels charge concerning thee: and in their hands they shall bear thee up, lest at any time thou dash thy foot against a stone.

Matthew 4:6

The Son of man shall send forth his angels, and they shall gather out of his kingdom all things that offend, and them which do iniquity;

Matthew 13:41

So shall it be at the end of the world: the angels shall come forth, and sever the wicked from among the just,

Matthew 13:49

For the Son of man shall come in the glory of his Father with his angels; and the he shall reward every man according to his works.

Matthew 16:27

Take heed that ye despise not one of these little ones; for I say unto you, That in heaven their angels do always behold the face of my Father which is in heaven.

Matthew 18:10

For in the resurrection they neither marry, nor are given in marriage, but are as the angels of God in heaven.

Matthews 22:30

And he shall send his angels with a great sound of a trumpet, and they shall gather his elect from the four winds, from one end of heaven to the other.

Matthew 24:31

Then shall he say also unto them on the left hand, Depart from me ye cursed, into everlasting fire, prepared for the devil and his angels:

Matthew 25:41

Thinkest thou that I cannot now pray to my Father, and he shall presently give me more than twelve legions of angels?

Matthew 26:53

But of that day and hour knoweth no man, no, not the angels of heaven, but my Father only.

Matthew 24:36

When the Son of man shall come in his glory, and all the holy angels with him, then shall he sit upon the throne of his glory:

Matthew 25:31

And, behold, there was a great earthquake: for the angel of the Lord descended from heaven, and came and rolled back the stone from the door, and sat upon it.

Matthew 28:2

And the angel answered and said unto women, Fear not ye: for I know that ye seek Jesus, which was crucified.

Matthew 28:5

He which testifieth these
things saith,
Surely I come quickly.
Amen.
Even so, come, Lord Jesus.
The grace of our Lord Jesus
Christ be with you all.
Amen

Revelation 22: 20-21

www.ingramcontent.com/pod-product-compliance
Lightning Source LLC
LaVergne TN
LVHW061529070526
838199LV00009B/428